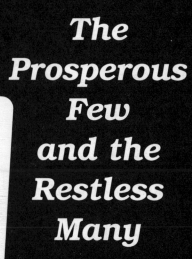

The Prosperous Few and the Restless Many

Noam Chomsky

Interviewed by David Barsamian

Odonian Press
Berkeley, California

Additional copies of this book and others in the Real Story series are available for $5 + $2 shipping per order (not per book) from Odonian Press, Box 7776, Berkeley CA 94707. To order by credit card, or for information on quantity discounts, please call us at 510 524 4000 or 800 REAL STORY. Distribution to book stores and book wholesalers is through Publishers Group West, Box 8843, Emeryville CA 94662, 510 658 3453 (toll-free: 800 788 3123).

Original compilation: David Barsamian

Condensation and reorganization: Sandy Niemann

Copyediting and proofreading: Karen Faria, Sandy Niemann, Arthur Naiman, Derek Stordahl, John Kadyk, Susan McCallister

Final edit, inside design, page layout and index:
Arthur Naiman

Cover photograph: Elaine Brière

Cover design for series: Studio Silicon

Layout and copy for this cover: Arthur Naiman, Karen Faria

Series editor: Arthur Naiman

Printing: Michelle Selby, Jim Puzey, Larry Hawkins / Consolidated Printers, Berkeley, California

---

Odonian Press gets its name from Ursula Le Guin's wonderful novel *The Dispossessed* (though we have no connection with Ms. Le Guin or any of her publishers). The last story in her collection *The Wind's Twelve Quarters* also features the Odonians.

Odonian Press donates at least 10% (last year it was 19%) of its aftertax income to organizations working for social justice.

Contents

Introduction

This book was compiled from three interviews I conducted with Noam Chomsky in the Boston area on December 16, 1992 and January 14 and 21, 1993, which were then edited and revised.

My questions appear in italics in this typeface. We've tried to define terms or names that may be unfamiliar the first time they occur. These explanations appear in this typeface [in square brackets].

Tapes and transcripts of hundreds of Chomsky's interviews and talks—and those of many other interesting speakers—are also available. For a free catalog, call 303-444-8788 or write me at 2129 Mapleton, Boulder CO 80304.

David Barsamian

About the author

Noam Chomsky was born in Philadelphia in 1928. Since 1955, he's taught at the Massachusetts Institute of Technology, where he became a full professor at the age of 32.

A major figure in 20th-century linguistics, Chomsky has also written many books on contemporary issues (see pp. 87–89). His political talks have been heard, typically by standing-room-only audiences, all over the country and the globe, and he's received countless honors and awards.

In a saner world, his tireless efforts to promote justice would have long since won him the Nobel Peace Prize, but the committee keeps giving it to people like Henry Kissinger.

Arthur Naiman

The new global economy

I was on Brattle Street [in Cambridge] *just last night. There were panhandlers, people asking for money, people sleeping in the doorways of buildings. This morning, in the subway station at Harvard Square, there was more of the same.*

The spectre of poverty and despair has become increasingly obvious to the middle and upper class. You just can't avoid it as you could years ago, when it was limited to a certain section of town. This has a lot to do with the pauperization (the internal Third Worldization, I think you call it) of the United States.

There are several factors involved. About twenty years ago there was a big change in the world order, partly symbolized by Richard Nixon's dismantling of the postwar economic system. He recognized that US dominance of the global system had declined, and that in the new "tripolar" world order (with Japan and German-based Europe playing a larger role), the US could no longer serve—in effect—as the world's banker.

That led to a lot more pressure on corporate profits in the US and, consequently, to a big attack on social welfare gains. The crumbs that were permitted to ordinary people had to be taken away. Everything had to go to the rich.

There was also a tremendous expansion of unregulated capital in the world. In 1971, Nixon dismantled the Bretton Woods system, thereby deregulating currencies. That, and a number of other changes, tremendously expanded the amount of unregulated capital in the world, and accelerated what's called the globalization (or the internationalization) of the economy.

That's a fancy way of saying that you export jobs to high-repression, low-wage areas—which undercuts the opportunities for productive labor at home. It's a way of increasing corporate profits, of course. And it's much easier to do with a free flow of capital, advances in telecommunications, etc.

There are two important consequences of globalization. First, it extends the Third World model to industrial countries. In the Third World, there's a two-tiered society—a sector of extreme wealth and privilege, and a sector of huge misery and despair among useless, superfluous people.

That division is deepened by the policies dictated by the West. It imposes a neoliberal "free market" system that directs resources to the wealthy and to foreign investors, with the idea that something will trickle down by magic, some time after the Messiah comes.

You can see this happening everywhere in the industrial world, but most strikingly in the three English-speaking countries. In the 1980s, England under Thatcher, the United States under the Reaganites and Australia under a Labor government adopted some of the doctrines they preached for the Third World.

Of course, they would never really play this game completely. It would be too harmful to the rich. But they flirted with it. And they suffered. That is, the general population suffered.

Take, for example, South Central Los Angeles. It had factories once. They moved to Eastern Europe, Mexico, Indonesia—where you can get peasant women flocking off the land.

But the rich did fine, just like they do in the Third World.

The second consequence, which is also important, has to do with governing structures. Throughout history, the structures of government have tended to coalesce around other forms of power—in modern times, primarily around economic power. So, when you have national economies, you get national states. We now have an international economy and we're moving towards an international state—which means, finally, an international executive.

To quote the business press, we're creating "a new imperial age" with a "de facto world government." It has its own institutions—like the International Monetary Fund (IMF) and the World Bank, trading structures like NAFTA and GATT [the North American Free Trade Agreement and the General Agreement on Tariffs and Trade, both discussed in the next section], executive meetings like the G-7 [the seven richest industrial countries—the US, Canada, Japan, Germany, Britain, France and Italy—who meet regularly to discuss economic policy] and the European Community bureaucracy.

As you'd expect, this whole structure of decision making answers basically to the transnational corporations, international banks, etc. It's also an effective blow against democracy. All these structures raise decision making to the executive level, leaving what's called a "democratic deficit"—parliaments and populations with less influence.

Not only that, but the general population doesn't know what's happening, and it doesn't even know that it doesn't know. One result is a kind of alienation from institutions. People feel that nothing works for them.

Sure it doesn't. They don't even know what's going on at that remote and secret level of decision making. That's a real success in the long-term task of depriving formal democratic structures of any substance.

At Clinton's Little Rock economic conference and elsewhere, there was much talk of economic recovery and restoring competitiveness. Political economist Gar Alperovitz wrote in the New York Times *that what's being proposed is "not likely to make a dent in our deeper economic problems. We may simply be in for a long, painful era of unresolved economic decay." Would you agree?*

I haven't seen that piece yet, but the *Financial Times* [of London, the world's leading business journal] has been talking with some pleasure of the fiscal conservatism shown by Clinton and his advisors.

There are serious issues here. First of all, we have to be careful in the use of terms. When someone says America is in for a long period of decline, we have to decide what we mean by "America." If we mean the geographical area of the United States, I'm sure that's right. The policies now being discussed will have only a cosmetic effect. There has been decline and there will be further decline. The country is acquiring many of the characteristics of a Third World society.

But if we're talking about US-based corporations, then it's probably not right. In fact, the indications are to the contrary—their share in manufacturing production, for example, has been stable or is probably even increasing, while the share of the US itself has declined. That's an automatic consequence of sending productive labor elsewhere.

General Motors, as the press constantly reports, is closing some 24 factories in North America. But in the small print you read that it's opening new factories—including, for example, a $700 million high-tech factory in East Germany. That's an area of huge unemployment where GM can pay 40% of the wages of Western Europe and none of the benefits.

There was a nice story on the front page of the *Financial Times*, in which they described what a great idea this was. As they put it, GM doesn't have to worry about the "pampered" West European workers any longer—they can just get highly exploited workers now that East Germany is being pushed back to its traditional Third World status. It's the same in Mexico, Thailand, etc.

The prescription for our economic problems is more of the same—"leave it to the market." There's such endless trumpeting of the free market that it assumes almost a myth-like quality. "It'll correct the problems." Are there any alternatives?

We have to first separate ideology from practice, because to talk about a free market at this point is something of a joke. Outside of ideologues, the academy and the press, no one thinks that capitalism is a viable system, and nobody has thought that for sixty or seventy years—if ever.

Herman Daly and Robert Goodland, two World Bank economists, circulated an interesting study recently. In it they point out that received economic theory—the standard theory on which decisions are supposed to be based—pictures a free market sea with tiny little islands of individual firms. These islands, of course, aren't internally free—they're centrally managed.

But that's okay, because these are just tiny little islands on the sea. We're supposed to believe that these firms aren't much different than a mom-and-pop store down the street.

Daly and Goodland point out that by now the islands are approaching the scale of the sea. A large percentage of cross-border transactions are within a single firm, hardly "trade" in any meaningful sense. What you have is centrally managed transactions, with a very visible hand—major corporate structures—directing it. And we have to add a further point—that the sea itself bears only a partial resemblance to free trade.

So you could say that one alternative to the free market system is the one we already have, because we often don't rely on the market where powerful interests would be damaged. Our actual economic policy is a mixture of protectionist, interventionist, free market and liberal measures. And it's directed primarily to the needs of those who implement social policy, who are mostly the wealthy and the powerful.

For example, the US has always had an active state industrial policy, just like every other industrial country. It's been understood that a system of private enterprise can survive only if there is extensive government intervention. It's needed to regulate disorderly markets and protect private capital from the destructive effects of the market system, and to organize a public subsidy for targeting advanced sectors of industry, etc.

But nobody *called* it industrial policy, because for half a century it has been masked within the Pentagon system. Internationally, the Pentagon was an intervention force, but domestically it was a method by which the government could coordinate the private economy, provide welfare to major corporations, subsidize them, arrange the flow of taxpayer money to research and development, provide a state-guaranteed market for excess production, target advanced industries for development, etc. Just about every successful and flourishing aspect of the US economy has relied on this kind of government involvement.

At the Little Rock conference I heard Clinton talking about structural problems and rebuilding the infrastructure. One attendee, Ann Markusen, a Rutgers economist and author of the book Dismantling the Cold War Economy, *talked about the excesses of the Pentagon system and the distortions and damages that it has caused to the US economy. So it seems that there's at least some discussion of these issues, which is something I don't recall ever before.*

The reason is that they can't maintain the Pentagon-based system as readily as before. They've got to start talking about it, because the mask is dropping. It's very difficult now to get people to lower their consumption or their aspirations in order to divert investment funds to high-technology industry on the pretext that the Russians are coming.

So the system is in trouble. Economists and bankers have been pointing out openly for some time that one of the main reasons why the current recovery is so sluggish is that the government hasn't been able to resort to increased military spending with all of its multiplier effects—the traditional pump-priming mechanism of economic stimulation. Although there are various efforts to continue this (in my opinion, the current operation in Somalia is one such effort to do some public relations work for the Pentagon), it's just not possible the way it used to be.

There's another fact to consider. The cutting edge of technology and industry has for some time been shifting in another direction, away from the electronics-based industry of the postwar period and towards biology-based industry and commerce.

Biotechnology, genetic engineering, seed and drug design (even designing animal species), etc. is expected to be a huge growth industry with enormous profits. It's potentially vastly more important than electronics—in fact, compared to the potential of biotechnology (which may extend to the essentials of life), electronics is sort of a frill.

But it's hard to disguise government involvement in these areas behind the Pentagon cover. Even if the Russians were still there, you couldn't do that.

There are differences between the two political parties about what should be done. The Reagan-Bush types, who are more fanatically ideological, have their heads in the sand about it to some extent. They are a bit more dogmatic. The Clinton people are more up front about these needs. That's one of the main reasons why Clinton had substantial business support.

Take the question of "infrastructure" or "human capital"—a kind of vulgar way of saying keep people alive and allow them to have an education. By now the business community is well aware that they've got problems with that.

The *Wall Street Journal*, for example, was the most extreme advocate of Reaganite lunacies for ten years. They're now publishing articles in which they're bemoaning the consequences—without, of course, conceding that they're consequences.

They had a big news article on the collapse of California's educational system, which they're very upset about. Businessmen in the San Diego area have relied on the state system—on a public subsidy—to provide them with skilled workers, junior managers, applied research, etc. Now the system is in collapse.

The reason is obvious—the large cutbacks in social spending in the federal budget, and the fiscal and other measures that greatly increased the federal debt (which the *Wall Street Journal* supported), simply transferred the burden of keeping people alive and functioning to the states. The states are unable to support that burden. They're in serious trouble and have tried to hand down the problem to the munici-palities, which are also in serious trouble.

The same is true if you're a rich business-man living in a rich suburb here in the Boston area. You would like to be able to get into your limousine and drive downtown and have a road. But the road has potholes. That's no good. You also want to be able to walk around the city and go to the theater without getting knifed.

So now businessmen are complaining. They want the government to get back into the business of providing them with what they need. That's going to mean a reversal of the fanaticism that the *Wall Street Journal* and others like it have been applauding all these years.

Talking about it is one thing, but do they really have a clue about what to do?

I think they do have a clue. If you listen to smart economists like Bob Solow, who started the Little Rock conference off, they have some pretty reasonable ideas.

What they want to do is done openly by Japan and Germany and every functioning economy—namely, rely on government initiatives to provide the basis for private profit. In the periphery of Japan—for example in South Korea and Taiwan—we've been seeing a move out of the Third World pattern to an industrial society through massive state intervention.

Not only is the state there powerful enough to control labor, but it's powerful enough to control capital. In the 1980s, Latin America had a huge problem of capital flight because they're open to international capital markets. South Korea has no such problem—they have the death penalty for capital flight. Like any sane planners, they use market systems for allocating resources, but very much under planned central direction.

The US has been doing it indirectly through the Pentagon system, which is kind of inefficient. It won't work as well any more anyway, so they'd like to do it openly. The question is whether that can be done. One problem is that the enormous debt created during the Reagan years—at the federal, state, corporate, local and even household levels—makes it extremely difficult to launch constructive programs.

There's no capital available.

That's right. In fact, that was probably part of the purpose of the Reaganite borrow-and-spend program.

To eliminate capital?

Recall that about ten years ago, when David Stockman [director of the Office of Management and Budget in the early Reagan years] was kicked out, he had some interviews with economic journalist William Greider. There Stockman pretty much said that the idea was to try to put a cap on social spending, simply by debt. There would always be plenty to subsidize the rich. But they wouldn't be able to pay aid to mothers with dependent children—only aid to dependent corporate executives.

Incidentally, the debt itself, just the numbers, may not be such a huge problem. We've had bigger debts than that—not in numbers, but relative to the GNP [the gross national product]—in the past. The exact amount of the debt is a bit of a statistical artifact. You can make it different things depending on how you count. Whatever it is, it's not something that couldn't be dealt with.

The question is—what was done with the borrowing? If the borrowing in the last ten years had been used for constructive purposes—say for investment or infrastructure—we'd be quite well off. But the borrowing was used for enrichment of the rich—for consumption (which meant lots of imports, building up the trade deficit), financial manipulation and speculation. All of these are very harmful to the economy.

There's another problem, a cultural and ideological problem. The government has for years relied on a propaganda system that denies these truths. It's other countries that have government involvement and social services—we're rugged individualists. So IBM doesn't get anything from the government. In fact, they get plenty, but it's through the Pentagon.

The propaganda system has also whipped up hysteria about taxation (though we're undertaxed by comparative standards) and about bureaucracies that interfere with profits—say, by protecting worker and consumer interests. Pointy-headed bureaucrats who funnel a public subsidy to industry and banks are just fine, of course.

Propaganda aside, the population *is*, by comparative standards, pretty individualistic and kind of dissident and doesn't take orders very well, so it's not going to be easy to sell state industrial policy to people. These cultural factors are significant.

In Europe there's been a kind of social contract. It's now declining, but it has been largely imposed by the strength of the unions, the organized work force and the relative weakness of the business community (which, for historical reasons, isn't as dominant in Europe as it has been here). European governments do see primarily to the needs of private wealth, but they also have created a not insubstantial safety net for the rest of the population. They have general health care, reasonable services, etc.

We haven't had that, in part because we don't have the same organized work force, and we have a much more class-conscious and dominant business community.

Japan achieved pretty much the same results as Europe, but primarily because of the highly authoritarian culture. People just do what they're told. So you tell them to cut back consumption—they have a very low standard of living, considering their wealth—work hard, etc. and people just do it. That's not so easy to do here.

Given the economic situation, it would seem to be a propitious moment for the left, the progressive movement, to come forward with some concrete proposals. Yet the left seems to be either bogged down in internecine warfare or in a reactive mode. It's not proactive.

What people call the "left" (the peace and justice movements, whatever they are) has expanded a lot over the years. They tend to be very localized. On particular issues they focus and achieve things.

But there's not much of a broader vision, or of institutional structure. The left can't coalesce around unions because the unions are essentially gone. To the extent that there's any formal structure, it's usually something like the church.

There's virtually no functioning left intelligentsia [intellectuals viewed as a distinct group or class]. Nobody's talking much about what should be done, or is even available to give talks. The class warfare of the last decades has been fairly successful in weakening popular organizations. People are isolated.

I should also say that the policy issues that have to be faced are quite deep. It's always nice to have reforms. It would be nice to have more money for starving children. But there are some objective problems which you and I would have to face if we ran the country.

One problem was kindly pointed out to the Clinton administration by a front page article in the *Wall Street Journal* the other day. It mentioned what might happen if the administration gets any funny ideas about taking some of their own rhetoric seriously—like spending money for social programs. (Granted, that's not very likely, but just in case anybody has some funny ideas.)

The United States is so deeply in hock to the international financial community (because of the debt) that they have a lock on US policy. If something happens here—say, increasing workers' salaries—that the bondholders don't like and will cut down their short-term profit, they'll just start withdrawing from the US bond market.

That will drive interest rates up, which will drive the economy down, which will increase the deficit. The *Journal* points out that Clinton's twenty-billion-dollar spending program could be turned into a twenty-billion-dollar cost to the government, to the debt, just by slight changes in the purchase and sale of bonds.

So social policy, even in a country as rich and powerful as the United States (which is the richest and most powerful of them all), is mortgaged to the international wealthy sectors here and abroad. Those are issues that have to be dealt with—and that means facing problems of revolutionary change.

There are doubtless many debates over this issue. All those debates assume that investors have the right to decide what happens. So we have to make things as attractive as possible to them. But as long as the investors have the right to decide what happens, nothing much is going to change.

It's like trying to decide whether to change from proportional representation to some other kind of representation in the state-run parliament of a totalitarian state. That might change things a little, but it's not going to matter much.

Until you get to the source of power, which ultimately is investment decisions, other changes are cosmetic and can only take place in a limited way. If they go too far, the investors will just make other choices, and there's nothing much you can do about it.

To challenge the right of investors to determine who lives, who dies, and how they live and die—that would be a significant move toward Enlightenment ideals (actually the classical liberal ideal). That would be revolutionary.

I'd like you to address another factor at work here. Psychologically, it's a lot easier to criticize something than to promote something constructive. There's a completely different dynamic at work.

You can see a lot of things that are wrong. Small changes you can propose. But to be realistic, substantial change (which will really alter the large-scale direction of things and overcome major problems) will require profound democratization of the society and the economic system.

A business or a big corporation is a fascist structure internally. Power is at the top. Orders go from top to bottom. You either follow the orders or get out.

The concentration of power in such structures means that everything in the ideological or political domains is sharply constrained. It's not totally controlled, by any means. But it's sharply constrained. Those are just facts.

The international economy imposes other kinds of constraints. You can't overlook those things—they're just true. If anybody bothered to read Adam Smith instead of prating about him, they'd see he pointed out that social policy is class-based. He took the class analysis for granted.

If you studied the canon properly at the University of Chicago [home of Milton Friedman and other right-wing economists], you learned that Adam Smith denounced the mercantilist system and colonialism because he was in favor of free trade. That's only half the truth. The other half is that he pointed out that the mercantilist system and colonialism were very beneficial to the "merchants and manufacturers...the principal architects of policy" but were harmful to the people of England.

In short, it was a class-based policy which worked for the rich and powerful in England. The people of England paid the costs. He was opposed to that because he was an enlightened intellectual, but he recognized it. Unless you recognize it, you're just not in the real world.

NAFTA and GATT—who benefits?

The last US-based typewriter company, Smith Corona, is moving to Mexico. There's a whole corridor of maquiladoras [factories where parts made elsewhere are assembled at low wages] *along the border. People work for five dollars a day, and there are incredible levels of pollution, toxic waste, lead in the water, etc.*

One of the major issues before the country right now is the North American Free Trade Agreement. There's no doubt that NAFTA's going to have very large effects on both Americans and Mexicans. You can debate what the effect will be, but nobody doubts that it'll be significant.

Quite likely the effect will be to accelerate just what you've been describing—a flow of productive labor to Mexico. There's a brutal and repressive dictatorship there, so it's guaranteed wages will be low.

During what's been called the "Mexican economic miracle" of the last decade, their wages have dropped 60%. Union organizers get killed. If the Ford Motor Company wants to toss out its work force and hire super cheap labor, they just do it. Nobody stops them. Pollution goes on unregulated. It's a great place for investors.

One might think that NAFTA, which includes sending productive labor down to Mexico, might improve their real wages, maybe level the two countries. But that's most unlikely. One reason is that the repression there prevents organizing for higher wages. Another reason is that NAFTA will flood Mexico with industrial agricultural products from the United States.

These products are all produced with big public subsidies, and they'll undercut Mexican agriculture. Mexico will be flooded with American crops, which will contribute to driving an estimated thirteen million people off the land to urban areas or into the *maquiladora* areas—which will again drive down wages.

NAFTA will very likely be quite harmful for American workers too. We may lose hundreds of thousands of jobs, or lower the level of jobs. Latino and black workers are the ones who are going to be hurt most.

But it'll almost certainly be a big bonanza for investors in the United States and for their counterparts in the wealthy sectors in Mexico. They're the ones—along with the professional classes who work for them—who are applauding the agreement.

Will NAFTA and GATT essentially formalize and institutionalize relations between the North [prosperous, industrialized, mostly northern nations] *and the South* [poorer, less industrialized, mostly southern nations]?

That's the idea. NAFTA will also almost certainly degrade environmental standards. For example, corporations will be able to argue that EPA [Environmental Protection Agency] standards are violations of free-trade agreements. This is already happening in the Canada-US part of the agreement. Its general effect will be to drive life down to the lowest level while keeping profits high.

It's interesting to see how the issue has been handled. The public hasn't the foggiest idea what's going on. In fact, they can't know. One reason is that NAFTA is effectively a secret—it's an executive agreement that isn't publicly available.

In 1974, the Trade Act was passed by Congress. One of its provisions was that the Labor Advisory Committee—which is based in the unions—had to have input and analysis on any trade-related issue. Obviously that committee had to report on NAFTA, which was an executive agreement signed by the president.

The Labor Advisory Committee was notified in mid-August 1992 that their report was due on September 9, 1992. However, they weren't given a text of the agreement until about 24 hours before the report was due. That meant they couldn't even convene, and they obviously couldn't write a serious report in time.

Now these are conservative labor leaders, not the kind of guys who criticize the government much. But they wrote a very acid report. They said that, to the extent that we can look at this in the few hours given to us, it looks like it's going to be a disaster for working people, for the environment, for Mexicans—and a great boon for investors.

The committee pointed out that although treaty advocates said it won't hurt many American workers, maybe just unskilled workers, their definition of "unskilled worker" would include 70% of the workforce. The committee also pointed out that property rights were being protected all over the place, but workers' rights were scarcely mentioned. The committee then bitterly condemned the utter contempt for democracy that was demonstrated by not giving the committee the complete text ahead of time.

GATT is the same—nobody knows what's going on there unless they're some kind of specialist. And GATT is even more far-reaching. One of the things being pressed very hard in those negotiations is what's called "intellectual property rights." That means protection for patents—also things like software, records, etc. The idea is to guarantee that the technology of the future remains in the hands of multinational corporations, for whom the world government works.

You want to make sure, for example, that India can't produce drugs for its population at 10% the cost of drugs produced by Merck Pharmaceutical, which is government supported and subsidized. Merck relies extensively on research that comes out of university biology laboratories (which are supported by public funds) and on all sorts of other forms of government intervention.

Have you seen details of these treaties?

By now it's theoretically possible to get a text. But what I've seen is the secondary comment on the text, like the Labor Advisory Committee report, and the report of the Congressional Office of Technology Assessment, which is fairly similar.

The crucial point is that even if you and I could get a text, what does that mean for American democracy? How many people even know that this is going on? The Labor Advisory Committee report, and the fact that the treaty was withheld from the Committee, was never even reported by the press (to my knowledge).

I just came back from a couple of weeks in Europe, where GATT is a pretty big issue for the people in the countries of the European Community. They're concerned about the gap that's developing between executive decisions (which are secret) and democratic (or at least partially democratic) institutions like parliaments, which are less and less able to influence decisions made at the Community level.

It seems that the Clinton-Gore Administration is going to be in a major conflict. It supports NAFTA and GATT, while at the same time talking—at least rhetorically—about its commitment to environmental protection and creating jobs for Americans.

I would be very surprised if there's a big conflict over that. I think your word "rhetorically" is accurate. Their commitment is to US-based corporations, which means transnational corporations. They approve of the form NAFTA is taking—special protection for property rights, but no protection for workers' rights—and the methods being developed to undercut environmental protection. That's in their interests. I doubt that there'll be a conflict in the administration unless there's a lot of public pressure.

Food and Third World "economic miracles"

Talk about the political economy of food, its production and distribution, particularly within the framework of IMF and World Bank policies. These institutions extend loans under very strict conditions to the nations of the South: they have to promote the market economy, pay back the loans in hard currency and increase exports—like coffee, so that we can

*drink cappuccino, or beef, so that we can eat ham-
burgers—at the expense of indigenous agriculture.*

You've described the basic picture. It's also
interesting to have a close look at the individual
cases. Take Bolivia. It was in trouble. There'd
been brutal, highly repressive dictators, huge
debt—the whole business.

The West went in—Jeffrey Sachs, a leading
Harvard expert, was the advisor—with the IMF
rules: stabilize the currency, increase agro-
export, cut down production for domestic needs,
etc. It worked. The figures, the macroeconomic
statistics, looked quite good. The currency has
been stabilized. The debt has been reduced. The
GNP has been increasing.

But there are a few flies in the ointment.
Poverty has rapidly increased. Malnutrition has
increased. The educational system has collapsed. But the most interesting thing is what's
stabilized the economy—exporting coca [the
plant from which cocaine is made]. It now accounts
for about two-thirds of Bolivian exports, by
some estimates.

The reason is obvious. Take a peasant farmer
somewhere and flood his area with US-subsi-
dized agriculture—maybe through a Food for
Peace program—so he can't produce or compete.
Set up a situation in which he can only function
as an agricultural exporter. He's not an idiot.
He's going to turn to the most profitable crop,
which happens to be coca.

The peasants, of course, don't get much
money out of this, and they also get guns and
DEA [the US Drug Enforcement Agency] helicopters.

But at least they can survive. And the world gets a flood of coca exports.

The profits mostly go to big syndicates or, for that matter, to New York banks. Nobody knows how many billions of dollars of cocaine profits pass through New York banks or their offshore affiliates, but it's undoubtedly plenty.

Plenty of it also goes to US-based chemical companies which, as is well known, are exporting the chemicals used in cocaine production to Latin America. So there's plenty of profit. It's probably giving a shot in the arm to the US economy as well. And it's contributing nicely to the international drug epidemic, including here in the US.

That's the economic miracle in Bolivia. And that's not the only case. Take a look at Chile. There's another big economic miracle. The poverty level has increased from about 20% during the Allende years [Salvador Allende, a democratically elected Socialist president of Chile, was assassinated in a US-backed military coup in 1973] up to about 40% now, after the great miracle. And that's true in country after country.

These are the kinds of consequences that will follow from what has properly been called "IMF fundamentalism." It's having a disastrous effect everywhere it's applied.

But from the point of view of the perpetrators, it's quite successful. As you sell off public assets, there's lots of money to be made, so much of the capital that fled Latin America is now back. The stock markets are doing nicely. The professionals and businessmen are very happy with it. And they're the ones who make the plans, write the articles, etc.

And now the same methods are being applied in Eastern Europe. In fact, the same people are going. After Sachs carried through the economic miracle in Bolivia, he went off to Poland and Russia to teach them the same rules.

You hear lots of praise for this economic miracle in the US too, because it's just a far more exaggerated version of what's happening here. The wealthy sector is doing fine, but the general public is in deep trouble. It's mild compared with the Third World, but the structure is the same.

Between 1985 and 1992, Americans suffering from hunger rose from twenty to thirty million. Yet novelist Tom Wolfe described the 1980s as one of the "great golden moments that humanity has ever experienced."

A couple of years ago Boston City Hospital— that's the hospital for the poor and the general public in Boston, not the fancy Harvard teaching hospital—had to institute a malnutrition clinic, because they were seeing it at Third World levels.

Most of the deep starvation and malnutrition in the US had pretty well been eliminated by the Great Society programs in the 1960s. But by the early 1980s it was beginning to creep up again, and now the latest estimates are thirty million or so in deep hunger.

It gets much worse over the winter because parents have to make an agonizing decision between heat and food, and children die because they're not getting water with some rice in it.

The group World Watch says that one of the solutions to the shortage of food is control of population. Do you support efforts to limit population?

First of all, there's no shortage of food. There are serious problems of distribution. That aside, I think there should be efforts to control population. There's a well-known way to do it—increase the economic level.

Population is declining very sharply in industrial societies. Many of them are barely reproducing their own population. Take Italy, which is a late industrializing country. The birth rate now doesn't reproduce the population. That's a standard phenomenon.

Coupled with education?

Coupled with education and, of course, the means for birth control. The United States has had a terrible role. It won't even help fund international efforts to provide education about birth control.

Photo ops in Somalia

Does Operation Restore Hope in Somalia represent a new pattern of US intervention in the world?

I don't think it really should be classified as an intervention. It's more of a public relations operation for the Pentagon.

In fact, it's intriguing that it was almost openly stated this time. Colin Powell, the [former] Chairman of the Joint Chiefs, made a statement about how this was a great public relations job for the military. A *Washington Post* editorial described it as a bonanza for the Pentagon.

The reporters could scarcely fail to see what was happening. After all, when the Pentagon calls up all the news bureaus and major television networks and says: "Look, be at such-and-such a beach at such-and-such an hour with your cameras aiming in this direction because you're going to watch Navy Seals climbing out of the water and it will be real exciting," nobody can fail to see that this is a PR job. That would be a level of stupidity that's too much for anyone.

The best explanation for the "intervention," in my opinion, was given in an article in the London *Financial Times* on the day of the landing. It didn't mention Somalia—it was about the US recession and why the recovery is so sluggish.

It quoted various economists from investment firms and banks—guys that really care about the economy. The consensus was that the recovery is slow because the standard method of government stimulation—pump priming through the Pentagon system—simply isn't available to the extent that it's been in the past.

Bush put it pretty honestly in his farewell address when he explained why we intervened in Somalia and not Bosnia. What it comes down to is that in Bosnia somebody might shoot at us. In Somalia it's just a bunch of teenaged kids. We figure thirty thousand Marines can handle that.

The famine was pretty much over and fighting had declined. So it's photo opportunities, basically. One hopes it will help the Somalis more than harm them, but they're more or less incidental. They're just props for Pentagon public relations.

This has to be finessed by the press at the moment, because Somalia is not a pretty story. The US was the main support for Siad Barre, a kind of Saddam Hussein clone, from 1978 through 1990 (so it's not ancient history). He was tearing the country apart.

He destroyed the civil and social structures—in fact, laid the basis for what's happening now—and, according to Africa Watch [a human rights monitoring group based in Washington, DC], probably killed fifty or sixty thousand people. The US was, and may well be still, supporting him. The forces, mostly loyal to him, are being supported through Kenya, which is very much under US influence.

The US was in Somalia for a reason—the military bases there are part of the system aimed at the Gulf region. However, I doubt that that's much of a concern at this point. There are much more secure bases and more stable areas. What's needed now, desperately needed, is some way to prevent the Pentagon budget from declining.

When the press and commentators say the US has no interests there, that's taking a very narrow and misleading view. Maintaining the Pentagon system is a major interest for the US economy.

A Navy and Marine White Paper in September 1992 discussed the military's shift in focus from global threats to "regional challenges and opportunities," including "humanitarian assistance and nation-building efforts in the Third World."

That's always been the cover, but the military budget is mainly for intervention. In fact, even strategic nuclear forces were basically for intervention.

The US is a global power. It isn't like the Soviet Union, which used to carry out intervention right around its borders, where they had an overwhelming conventional force advantage. The US carried out intervention everywhere—in Southeast Asia, in the Middle East and in places where it had no such dominance. So the US had to have an extremely intimidating posture to make sure that nobody got in the way.

That required what was called a "nuclear umbrella"—powerful strategic weapons to intimidate everybody, so that conventional forces could be an instrument of political power. In fact, almost the entire military system—its military aspect, not its economic aspect—was geared for intervention. But that was often covered as "nation building." In Vietnam, in Central America—we're always humanitarian.

So when the Marine Corps documents say we now have a new mission—humanitarian nation building—that's just the old cover story. We now have to emphasize it more because traditional pretext—the conflict with the Russians—is gone, but it's the same as it's always been.

What kind of impact will the injection of US armed forces into Somalia have on the civil society? Somalia has been described by one US military official as "Dodge City" and the Marines as "Wyatt Earp." What happens when the marshal leaves town?

First of all, that description has little to do with Somalia. One striking aspect of this intervention is that there's no concern for Somalia. No one who knew anything about Somalia was involved in planning it, and there's no interaction with Somalis as far as we know (so far, at least).

Since the Marines have gone in, the only people they've dealt with are the so-called "warlords," and they're the biggest gangsters in the country. But Somalia is a *country*. There are people who know and care about it, but they don't have much of a voice here.

One of the most knowledgeable is a Somali woman named Rakiya Omaar, who was the Executive Director of Africa Watch. She did most of the human rights work, writing, etc. up until the intervention. She strongly opposed the intervention and was fired from Africa Watch.

Another knowledgeable voice is her co-director, Alex de Waal, who resigned from Africa Watch in protest after she was fired. In addition to his human rights work, he's an academic specialist on the region. He's written many articles and has published a major book on the Sudan famine with Oxford University Press. He knows not only Somalia but the region very well. And there are others. Their picture is typically quite different from the one we get here.

Siad Barre's main atrocities were in the northern part of Somalia, which had been a British colony. They were recovering from his US-backed attack and were pretty well organized (although they could, no doubt, have used aid). Their own civil society was emerging—a rather traditional one, with traditional elders, but with lots of new groups. Women's groups, for example, emerged in this crisis.

The area of real crisis was one region in the south. In part, that's because of General Mohammed Hersi's forces, which are supported from Kenya. (Hersi, who's known as Morgan, is Siad Barre's son-in-law.) His forces, as well as those of General Mohammed Farah Aidid and Ali Mahdi, were carrying out some of the worst atrocities. This led to a serious breakdown in which people just grabbed guns in order to survive. There was lots of looting, and teenaged gangsters.

By September–October [1992], that region was already recovering. Even though groups like US Care and the UN operations were extremely incompetent, other aid groups—like the International Red Cross, Save The Children, and smaller groups like the American Friends Service Committee or Australian Care—were getting most of the aid through.

By early November, 80–90% of their aid was reportedly getting through; by late November the figures were up to 95%. The reason was that they were working with the reconstituting Somalian society. In this southern corner of real violence and starvation, things were already recovering, just as they had in the north.

A lot of this had been under the initiative of a UN negotiator, Mohammed Sahnoun of Algeria, who was extremely successful and highly respected on all sides. He was working with traditional elders and the newly emerging civic groups, especially the women's groups, and they were coming back together under his guidance, or at least his initiative.

But Sahnoun was kicked out by [UN Secretary General] Boutros-Ghali in October because he publicly criticized the incompetence and corruption of the UN effort. The UN put in an Iraqi replacement, who apparently achieved very little.

A US intervention was apparently planned for shortly after the election. The official story is that it was decided upon at the end of November, when George Bush saw heart-rending pictures on television. But, in fact, US reporters in Baidoa in early November saw Marine officers in civilian clothes walking around and scouting out the area, planning for where they were going to set up their base.

This was rational timing. The worst crisis was over, the society was reconstituting and you could be pretty well guaranteed a fair success at getting food in, since it was getting in anyway. Thirty thousand troops would only expedite it in the short term. There wouldn't be too much fighting, because that was subsiding. So it wasn't Dodge City.

Bush got the photo opportunities and left somebody else to face the problems that were bound to arise later on. Nobody cared what happens to the Somalis. If it works, great, we'll applaud and cheer ourselves and bask in self-acclaim. If it turns into a disaster, we'll treat it the same as other interventions that turn into disasters.

After all, there's a long series of them. Take Grenada. That was a humanitarian intervention. We were going to save the people from tragedy and turn it into what Reagan called a "showplace for democracy" or a "showplace for capitalism."

The US poured aid in. Grenada had the highest per capita aid in the world the following year—next to Israel, which is in another category. And it turned into a complete disaster.

The society is in total collapse. About the only thing that's functioning there is money laundering for drugs. But nobody hears about it. The television cameras were told to look somewhere else.

So if the Marine intervention turns out to be a success, which is conceivable, then there'll be plenty of focus on it and how marvelous we are. If it turns into a disaster, it's off the map—forget about it. Either way we can't lose.

Slav vs. Slav

Would you comment on the events in the former Yugoslavia, which constitute the greatest outburst of violence in Europe in fifty years—tens of thousands killed, hundreds of thousands of refugees. This isn't some remote place like East Timor we're talking about—this is Europe—and it's on the news every night.

In a certain sense, what's happening is that the British and American right wings are getting what they asked for. Since the 1940s they've been quite bitter about the fact that Western support turned to Tito and the partisans, and against Mikailhovich and his Chetniks, and the Croatian anti-Communists, including the Ustasha, who were outright Nazis. The Chetniks were also playing with the Nazis and were trying to overcome the partisans.

The partisan victory imposed a communist dictatorship, but it also federated the country. It suppressed the ethnic violence that had accompanied the hatreds and created the basis of some sort of functioning society in which the parts had their role. We're now essentially back in the 1940s, but without the partisans.

Serbia is the inheritor of the Chetniks and their ideology. Croatia is the inheritor of the Ustasha and its ideology (less ferocious than the Nazi original, but similar). It's possible that they're now carrying out pretty much what they would've done if the partisans hadn't won.

Of course, the leadership of these elements comes from the Communist party, but that's because every thug in the region went into the ruling apparatus. (Yeltsin, for example, was a Communist party boss.)

It's interesting that the right wing in the West—at least its more honest elements—defend much of what's happening. For example, Nora Beloff, a right-wing British commentator on Yugoslavia, wrote a letter to the London *Economist* condemning those who denounce the Serbs in Bosnia. She's saying it's the fault of the Muslims. They're refusing to accommodate the Serbs, who are just defending themselves.

She's been a supporter of the Chetniks from way back, so there's no reason why she shouldn't continue to support Chetnik violence (which is what this amounts to). Of course there may be another factor. She's an extremist Zionist, and the fact that the Muslims are involved already makes them guilty.

Some say that, just as the Allies should have bombed the rail lines to Auschwitz to prevent the deaths of many people in concentration camps, so

*we should now bomb the Serbian gun positions sur-
rounding Sarajevo that have kept that city under
siege. Would you advocate the use of force?*

First of all, there's a good deal of debate about
how much effect bombing the rail lines to
Auschwitz would have had. Putting that aside, it
seems to me that a judicious threat and use of
force, not by the Western powers but by some
international or multinational group, might, at
an earlier stage, have suppressed a good deal of
the violence and maybe blocked it. I don't know
if it would help now.

If it were possible to stop the bombardment
of Sarajevo by threatening to bomb some
emplacements (and perhaps even carrying the
threat out), I think you could give an argument
for it. But that's a very big *if*. It's not only a
moral issue—you have to ask about the consequences, and they could be quite complex.

What if a Balkan war were set off? One consequence is that conservative military forces
within Russia could move in. They're already
there, in fact, to support their Slavic brothers in
Serbia. They might move in *en masse*. (That's
traditional, incidentally. Go back to Tolstoy's
novels and read about how Russians were going
to the south to save their Slavic brothers from
attacks. It's now being reenacted.)

At that point you're getting fingers on nuclear
weapons involved. It's also entirely possible that
an attack on the Serbs, who feel that they're the
aggrieved party, could inspire them to move
more aggressively in Kosovo, the Albanian area.
That could set off a large-scale war, with Greece
and Turkey involved. So it's not so simple.

Or what if the Bosnian Serbs, with the backing of both the Serbian and maybe even other Slavic regions, started a guerrilla war? Western military "experts" have suggested it could take a hundred thousand troops just to more or less hold the area. Maybe so.

So one has to ask a lot of questions about consequences. Bombing Serbian gun emplacements sounds simple, but you have to ask how many people are going to end up being killed. That's not so simple.

Zeljko Raznjatovic, known as Arkan, a fugitive wanted for bank robbery in Sweden, was elected to the Serb Parliament in December 1992. His Tigers' Militia is accused of killing civilians in Bosnia. He's among ten people listed by the US State Department as a possible war criminal. Arkan dismissed the charges and said, "There are a lot of people in the United States I could list as war criminals."

That's quite correct. By the standards of Nuremberg, there are plenty of people who could be listed as war criminals in the West. It doesn't absolve him in any respect, of course.

The chosen country

The conditions of the US-Israel alliance have changed, but have there been any structural changes?

There haven't been any significant structural changes. It's just that the capacity of Israel to serve US interests, at least in the short term, has probably increased.

The Clinton administration has made it very clear that it intends to persist in the extreme pro-Israeli bias of the Bush administration. They've appointed Martin Indyk, whose background is in AIPAC [the American Israel Public Affairs Committee, a lobbying group], to the Middle East desk of the National Security Council.

He's headed a fraudulent research institute, the Washington Institute for Near East Studies. It's mainly there so that journalists who want to publish Israeli propaganda, but want to do it "objectively," can quote somebody who'll express what they want said.

The United States has always had one major hope from the so-called peace negotiations—that the traditional tacit alliance between Israel and the family dictatorships ruling the Gulf states will somehow become a little more overt or solidified. And it's conceivable.

There's a big problem, however. Israel's plans to take over and integrate what they want of the occupied territories—plans which have never changed—are running into some objective problems. Israel has always hoped that in the long run they would be able to expel much of the Palestinian population.

Many moves were made to accelerate that. One of the reasons they instituted an educational system on the West Bank was in hopes that more educated people would want to get out because there weren't any job opportunities.

For a long time it worked—they were able to get a lot of people to leave—but they now may well be stuck with the population. This is going to cause some real problems, because Israel intends to take the water and the usable land. That may not be so pretty or so easy.

What's Israel's record of compliance with the more than twenty Security Council resolutions condemning its policies?

It's in a class by itself.

No sanctions, no enforcement?

None. Just to pick one at random—Security Council Resolution 425, March 1978. It called on Israel to withdraw immediately and unconditionally from Lebanon. Israel is still there, even though the request was renewed by the government of Lebanon in February 1991, when everyone was going at Iraq.

The United States will block any attempt to change things. Many of the large number of Security Council resolutions vetoed by the US have to do with Israeli aggression or atrocities.

For example, take the invasion of Lebanon in 1982. At first the United States went along with the Security Council condemnations. But within a few days the US had vetoed the major Security Council resolution that called on everyone to withdraw and stop fighting, and later vetoed another, similar one.

The US has gone along with the last few UN resolutions or deportations.

The US has gone along, but has refused to allow them to have any teeth. The crucial question is: Does the US do anything about it? For example, the United States went along with the Security Council resolution condemning the annexation of the Golan Heights. But when the time came to do something about it, they refused.

International law transcends state law, but Israel says these resolutions are not applicable. How are they not applicable?

Just as international law isn't applicable to the United States, which has even been condemned by the World Court. States do what they feel like—though of course small states have to obey.

Israel's not a small state. It's an appendage to the world superpower, so it does what the United States allows. The United States tells it: You don't have to obey any of these resolutions, therefore they're null and void—just as they are when the US gets condemned.

The US never gets condemned by a Security Council resolution, because it vetoes them. Take the invasion of Panama. There were two resolutions in the Security Council condemning the United States for that invasion. We vetoed them both.

You can find repeated Security Council resolutions that never passed that condemn the US, ones which would have passed if they were about a defenseless country. And the General Assembly passes resolutions all the time, but they have no standing—they're just recommendations.

I remember talking to Mona Rishmawi, a lawyer for the human rights organization Al Haq in Ramallah on the West Bank. She told me that when she would go to court, she wouldn't know whether the Israeli prosecutor would prosecute her clients under British mandate emergency law, Jordanian law, Israeli law or Ottoman law.

Or their own laws. There are administrative regulations, some of which are never published. As any Palestinian lawyer will tell you, the legal system in the territories is a joke. There's no law—just pure authority.

Most of the convictions are based on confessions, and everybody knows what it means when people confess. Finally, after about sixteen years, a Druze Israeli army veteran who'd confessed and was sentenced was later proven to be innocent. Then it became a scandal.

There was an investigation, and the Supreme Court stated that for sixteen years the secret services had been lying to them. The secret services had been torturing people—as everybody knew—but telling the Court they weren't.

There was a big fuss about the fact that they'd been lying to the Supreme Court. How could you have a democracy when they lie to the Supreme Court? But the torture wasn't a big issue—everyone knew about it all along.

Amnesty International interviewed Supreme Court Justice Moshe Etzioni in London in 1977. They asked him to explain why such an extremely high percentage of Arabs confessed. He said, "It's part of their nature."

That's the Israeli legal system in the territories.

Explain these Orwellisms of "security zone" and "buffer zone."

In southern Lebanon? That's what Israel calls it, and that's how it's referred to in the media.

Israel invaded southern Lebanon in 1978. It was all in the context of the Camp David agreements. It was pretty obvious that those agreements would have the consequence they did—namely, freeing up Israel to attack Lebanon and integrate the occupied territories, now that Egypt was eliminated as a deterrent.

Israel invaded southern Lebanon and held onto it through clients—at the time it was Major Sa'ad Haddad's militia, basically an Israeli mercenary force. That's when Security Council Resolution 425 [described on page 41] was passed.

When Israel invaded in 1982, there'd been a lot of recent violence across the border, all from Israel north. There had been an American-brokered cease-fire which the PLO [the Palestine Liberation Organization] had held to scrupulously, initiating no cross-border actions. But Israel carried out thousands of provocative actions, including bombing of civilian targets—all to try to get the PLO to do something, thus giving Israel an excuse to invade.

It's interesting the way that period has been reconstructed in American journalism. All that remains is tales of the PLO's bombardment of Israeli settlements, a fraction of the true story (and in the year leading up to the 1982 Israeli invasion, not even that).

The truth was that Israel was bombing and invading north of the border, and the PLO wasn't responding. In fact, they were trying to move towards a negotiated settlement. (The truth about earlier years also has only a limited resemblance to the standard picture, as I've documented several times—uselessly, of course.)

We know what happened after Israel invaded Lebanon. They were driven out by what they call "terrorism"—meaning resistance by people who weren't going to be cowed. Israel succeeded in awakening a fundamentalist resistance, which it couldn't control. They were forced out.

They held on to the southern sector, which they call a "security zone"—although there's no reason to believe that it has the slightest thing to do with security. It's Israel's foothold in Lebanon. It's now run by a mercenary army, the South Lebanon Army, which is backed up by Israeli troops. They're very brutal. There are horrible torture chambers.

We don't know the full details, because they refuse to allow inspections by the Red Cross or anyone else. But there have been investigations by human rights groups, journalists and others. Independent sources—people who got out, plus some Israeli sources—overwhelmingly attest to the brutality. There was even an Israeli soldier who committed suicide because he couldn't stand what was going on. Some others have written about it in the Hebrew press.

Ansar is the main camp. They very nicely put it in the town of Khiyam. There was a massacre there by the Haddad militia under Israeli eyes in 1978, after years of Israeli bombing, that drove out most of the population. That's mainly for Lebanese who refuse to cooperate with the South Lebanon Army.

So that's the "security zone."

Israel dumped scores of deportees in Lebanon in the 1970s and 1980s. Why has that changed now? Why has Lebanon refused?

It's not so much that it has refused. If Israel dropped some deportees by helicopter into the outskirts of Sidon, Lebanon couldn't refuse. But this time I think Israel made a tactical error. The deportation of 415 Palestinians [in December 1992] is going to be very hard for them to deal with.

According to the Israeli press, this mass deportation was fairly random, a brutal form of collective punishment. I read in *Ha'aretz* [the leading Israeli newspaper] that the Shabak [the Israeli secret police] leaked the information that they had only given six names of security risks, adding a seventh when the Rabin Labor government wanted a larger number. The other four hundred or so were added by Rabin's government, without intelligence information.

So there's no reason to believe that those who were deported were Hamas [Islamic fundamentalist] activists. In fact, Israel deported virtually the whole faculty of one Islamic university. They essentially deported the intellectuals, people involved in welfare programs and so on.

But to take this big class of people and put them in the mountains of southern Lebanon, where it's freezing now and boiling hot in the summer—that's not going to look pretty in front of the TV cameras. And that's the only thing that matters. So there may be some problems, because Israel's not going to let them back in without plenty of pressure.

I heard Steven Solarz [former Democratic congressman from Brooklyn] *on the BBC. He said the world has a double standard: 700,000 Yemenis were expelled from Saudi Arabia and no one said a word (which is true); 415 Palestinians get expelled from Gaza and the West Bank and everybody's screaming.*

Every Stalinist said the same thing: "We sent Sakharov into exile and everyone was screaming. What about this or that other atrocity—which is worse?" There is always somebody who has committed a worse atrocity. For a Stalinist mimic like Solarz, why not use the same line?

Incidentally, there is a difference—the Yemenis were deported *to* their country, the Palestinians *from* their country. Would Solarz claim that we all should be silent if he and his family were dumped into a desert in Mexico?

Israel's record and its attitude toward Hamas have evolved over the years. Didn't Israel once favor it?

They not only favored it, they tried to organize and stimulate it. Israel was sponsoring Islamic fundamentalists in the early days of the *intifada* [the uprising of Palestinians within Israel against the Israeli government]. If there was a strike of students at some West Bank university, the Israeli army would sometimes bus in Islamic fundamentalists to break up the strike.

Sheikh Yaseen, an anti-Semitic maniac in Gaza and the leader of the Islamic fundamentalists, was protected for a long time. They liked him. He was saying, "Let's kill all the Jews." It's a standard thing, way back in history. Seventy years ago Chaim Weizmann was saying: Our danger is Arab moderates, not the Arab extremists.

The invasion of Lebanon was the same thing. Israel wanted to destroy the PLO because it was secular and nationalist, and was calling for negotiations and a diplomatic settlement. That was the threat, not the terrorists. Israeli commentators have been quite frank about that from the start.

Israel keeps making the same mistake, with the same predictable results. In Lebanon, they went in to destroy the threat of moderation and ended up with Hezbollah [Iranian-backed fundamentalists] on their hands. In the West Bank, they also wanted to destroy the threat of moderation—people who wanted to make a political settlement. There Israel's ending up with Hamas, which organizes effective guerrilla attacks on Israeli security forces.

It's important to recognize how utterly incompetent secret services are when it comes to dealing with people and politics. Intelligence agencies make the most astonishing mistakes— just as academics do.

In a situation of occupation or domination, the occupier, the dominant power, has to justify what it's doing. There is only one way to do it—become a racist. You have to blame the victim. Once you become a raving racist in self-defense, you've lost your capacity to understand what's happening.

The US in Indochina was the same. They never could understand—there are some amazing examples in the internal record. The FBI right here is the same—they make the most astonishing mistakes, for similar reasons.

In a letter to the New York Times, *Anti-Defamation League director Abraham Foxman wrote that the Rabin government has "unambiguously demonstrated its commitment to the peace process" since assuming leadership. "Israel is the last party that has to prove its desire to make peace." What's been the record of Rabin's Labor government?*

It's perfectly true that Israel wants peace. So did Hitler. Everybody wants peace. The question is, on what terms?

The Rabin government, exactly as was predicted, harshened the repression in the territories. Just this afternoon I was speaking to a woman who's spent the last couple of years in Gaza doing human rights work. She reported what everyone reports, and what everybody with a brain knows—as soon as Rabin came, it got tougher. He's the iron-fist man—that's his record.

Likud actually had a better record in the territories than Labor did. Torture and collective punishment stopped under Begin. There was one bad period when Sharon was in charge, but under Begin it was generally better. When the Labor party came back into the government in 1984, torture and collective punishment started again, and later the *intifada* came.

In February 1989, Rabin told a group of Peace Now leaders that the negotiations with the PLO didn't mean anything—they were going to give him time to crush the Palestinians by force. And they will be crushed, he said, they will be broken.

It hasn't happened.

It happened. The *intifada* was pretty much dead, and Rabin awakened it again with his own violence. He has also continued settlement in the occupied territories, exactly as everyone with their eyes open predicted. Although there was a very highly publicized settlement cutoff, it was clear right away that it was a fraud. Foxman knows that. He reads the Israeli press, I'm sure.

What Rabin stopped was some of the more extreme and crazy Sharon plans. Sharon was building houses all over the place, in places where nobody was ever going to go, and the country couldn't finance it. So Rabin eased back to a more rational settlement program. I think the current number is 11,000 new homes going up.

Labor tends to have a more rational policy than Likud—that's one of the reasons the US has always preferred Labor. They do pretty much the same things as Likud, but more quietly, less brazenly. They tend to be more modern in their orientation, better attuned to the norms of Western hypocrisy. Also, they're more realistic. Instead of trying to make seven big areas of settlement, they're down to four.

But the goal is pretty much the same—to arrange the settlements so that they separate the Palestinian areas. Big highway networks will connect Jewish settlements and surround some little Arab village way up in the hills. That's to make certain that any local autonomy will never turn into a form of meaningful self-government. All of this is continuing and the US is, of course, funding it.

Critics of the Palestinian movement point to what they call the "intrafada," the fact that Palestinians are killing other Palestinians—as if this justifies Israeli rule and delegitimizes Palestinian aspirations.

You might look back at the Zionist movement—there were plenty of Jews killed by other Jews. They killed collaborators, traitors and people they thought were traitors. And they weren't under anything like the harsh conditions of the

Palestinian occupation. As plenty of Israelis have pointed out, the British weren't nice, but they were gentlemen compared with us.

The Labor-based defense force Haganah had torture chambers and assassins. I once looked up their first recorded assassination in the official Haganah history. It's described there straight.

It was in 1921. A Dutch Jew named Jacob de Haan had to be killed, because he was trying to approach local Palestinians to see if things could be worked out between them and the new Jewish settlers. His murderer was assumed to be the woman who later became the wife of the first president of Israel. They said that another reason for assassinating him was that he was a homosexual.

Yitzhak Shamir became head of the Stern gang by killing the guy who was designated to be the head. He didn't like him for some reason. Shamir was supposed to take a walk with him on a beach. He never came back. Everyone knows Shamir killed him.

As the *intifada* began to self-destruct under tremendous repression, the killing got completely out of hand. It began to be a matter of settling old scores and gangsters killing anybody they saw. Originally the *intifada* was pretty disciplined, but it ended up with a lot of random killing, which Israel loves. Then they can point out how rotten the Arabs are.

It's a dangerous neighborhood.

Yes, it is. They help make it dangerous.

Gandhi, nonviolence and India

I've never heard you talk about Gandhi. Orwell wrote of him that, "Compared to other leading political figures of our times, how clean a smell he has managed to leave behind." What are your views on the Mahatma?

I'd hesitate to say without analyzing more closely what he did and what he achieved. There were some positive things—for example, his emphasis on village development, self-help and communal projects. That would have been very healthy for India. Implicitly, he was suggesting a model of development that could have been more successful and humane than the Stalinist model that was adopted (which emphasized the development of heavy industry, etc.).

But you really have to think through the talk about nonviolence. Sure, everybody's in favor of nonviolence rather than violence, but under what conditions and when? Is it an absolute principle?

You know what he said to Lewis Fisher in 1938 about the Jews in Germany—that German Jews ought to commit collective suicide, which would "have aroused the world and the people of Germany to Hitler's violence."

He was making a tactical proposal, not a principled one. He wasn't saying that they should have walked cheerfully into the gas chambers because that's what nonviolence dictates. He was saying, "if you do it, you may be better off."

If you divorce his proposal from any principled concern other than how many people's lives can be saved, it's conceivable that it would have aroused world concern in a way that the Nazi slaughter didn't. I don't believe it, but it's not literally impossible. On the other hand, there's nothing much that the European Jews could have done anyway under the prevailing circumstances, which were shameful everywhere.

Orwell adds that after the war Gandhi justified his position, saying, "The Jews had been killed anyway and might as well have died significantly."

Again, he was making a tactical, not a principled, statement. One has to ask what the consequences of the actions he recommended would have been. That's speculation based on little evidence. But for him to have made that recommendation at the time would have been grotesque.

What he should have been emphasizing is: "Look, powerless people who are being led to slaughter can't do anything. Therefore it's up to others to prevent them from being massacred." To give them advice on how they should be slaughtered isn't very uplifting—to put it mildly.

You can say the same about lots of other things. Take people being tortured and murdered in Haiti. You want to tell them: "The way you ought to do it is to walk up to the killers and put your head in front of their knife—and maybe people on the outside will notice." Could be. But it'd be a little more significant to tell the people who are giving the murderers the knives that they should do something better.

Preaching nonviolence is easy. One can take it seriously when it's someone like [long-time pacifist and activist] Dave Dellinger, who's right up front with the victims.

India today is torn asunder by various separatist movements. Kashmir is an incredible mess, occupied by the Indian army, and there are killings, detentions and massive human rights violations in the Punjab and elsewhere.

I'd like you to comment on a tendency in the Third World to blame the colonial masters for all the problems that are besetting their countries today. They seem to say, "Yes, India has problems, but it's the fault of the British—before that, India was just one happy place."

It's difficult to assess blame for historical disasters. It's somewhat like trying to assess blame for the health of a starving and diseased person. There are lots of different factors. Let's say the person was tortured—that certainly had an effect. But maybe when the torture was over, that person ate the wrong diet, lived a dissolute life and died from the combined effects. That's the kind of thing we're talking about.

There's no doubt that imperial rule was a disaster. Take India. When the British first moved into Bengal, it was one of the richest places in the world. The first British merchant warriors described it as a paradise. That area is now Bangladesh and Calcutta—the very symbols of despair and hopelessness.

There were rich agricultural areas producing unusually fine cotton. They also had advanced manufacturing, by the standards of the day. For example, an Indian firm built one of the flagships for an English admiral during the Napoleonic Wars. It wasn't built in British factories—it was the Indians' own manufacture.

You can read about what happened in Adam Smith, who was writing over two hundred years ago. He deplored the deprivations that the British were carrying out in Bengal. As he puts it, they first destroyed the agricultural economy and then turned "dearth into a famine." One way they did this was by taking the agricultural lands and turning them into poppy production (since opium was the only thing Britain could sell to China). Then there was mass starvation in Bengal.

The British also tried to destroy the existing manufacturing system in the parts of India they controlled. Starting from about 1700, Britain imposed harsh tariff regulations to prevent Indian manufacturers from competing with British textiles. They had to undercut and destroy Indian textiles because India had a comparative advantage. They were using better cotton and their manufacturing system was in many respects comparable to, if not better than, the British system.

The British succeeded. India deindustrialized, it ruralized. As the industrial revolution spread in England, India was turning into a poor, ruralized and agrarian country.

It wasn't until 1846, when their competitors had been destroyed and they were way ahead, that Britain suddenly discovered the merits of free trade. Read the British liberal historians, the big advocates of free trade—they were very well aware of it. Right through that period they say: "Look, what we're doing to India isn't pretty, but there's no other way for the mills of Manchester to survive. We have to destroy the competition."

And it continues. We can pursue this case by case through India. In 1944, Nehru wrote an interesting book *[The Discovery of India]* from a British prison. He pointed out that if you trace British influence and control in each region of India, and then compare that with the level of poverty in the region, they correlate. The longer the British have been in a region, the poorer it is. The worst, of course, was Bengal—now Bangladesh. That's where the British were first.

You can't trace these same things in Canada and North America, because there they just decimated the population. It's not only the current "politically correct" commentators that describe this—you can go right back to the founding fathers.

The first secretary of defense, General Henry Knox, said that what we're doing to the native population is worse than what the conquistadors did in Peru and Mexico. He said future historians will look at the "destruction" of these people—what would nowadays be called genocide—and paint the acts with "sable colors" [in other words, darkly].

This was known all the way through. Long after John Quincy Adams, the intellectual father of Manifest Destiny, left power, he became an opponent of both slavery and the policy toward the Indians. He said he'd been involved—along with the rest of them—in a crime of "extermination" of such enormity that surely God would punish them for these "heinous sins."

Latin America was more complex, but the initial population was virtually destroyed within a hundred and fifty years. Meanwhile, Africans were brought over as slaves. That helped devastate Africa even before the colonial period, then the conquest of Africa drove it back even further.

After the West had robbed the colonies—as they did, no question about that, and there's also no question that it contributed to their own development—they changed over to so-called "neocolonial" relationships, which means domination without direct administration. After that it was generally a further disaster.

Divide and conquer

To continue with India: talk about the divide-and-rule policy of the British Raj, playing off Hindus against Muslims. You see the results of that today.

Naturally, any conqueror is going to play one group against another. For example, I think about 90% of the forces that the British used to control India were Indians.

There's that astonishing statistic that at the height of British power in India, they never had more than 150,000 people there.

That was true everywhere. It was true when the American forces conquered the Philippines, killing a couple hundred thousand people. They were being helped by Philippine tribes, exploiting conflicts among local groups. There were plenty who were going to side with the conquerors.

But forget the Third World—just take a look at the Nazi conquest of nice, civilized Western

Europe, places like Belgium and Holland and France. Who was rounding up the Jews? Local people, often. In France they were rounding them up faster than the Nazis could handle them. The Nazis also used Jews to control Jews.

If the United States was conquered by the Russians, Ronald Reagan, George Bush, Elliott Abrams and the rest of them would probably be working for the invaders, sending people off to concentration camps. They're the right personality types.

That's the traditional pattern. Invaders quite typically use collaborators to run things for them. They very naturally play upon any existing rivalries and hostilities to get one group to work for them against others.

It's happening right now with the Kurds. The West is trying to mobilize Iraqi Kurds to destroy Turkish Kurds, who are by far the largest group and historically the most oppressed. Apart from what we might think of those guerrillas, there's no doubt that they had substantial popular support in southeastern Turkey.

(Turkey's atrocities against the Kurds haven't been covered much in the West, because Turkey is our ally. But right into the Gulf War they were bombing in Kurdish areas, and tens of thousands of people were driven out.)

Now the Western goal is to use the Iraqi Kurds as a weapon to try and restore what's called "stability"—meaning their own kind of system—in Iraq. The West is using the Iraqi Kurds to destroy the Turkish Kurds, since that will extend Turkey's power in the region, and the Iraqi Kurds are cooperating.

In October 1992, there was a very ugly incident in which there was a kind of pincers movement between the Turkish army and the Iraqi Kurdish forces to expel and destroy Kurdish guerrillas from Turkey.

Iraqi Kurdish leaders and some sectors of the population cooperated because they thought they could gain something by it. You could understand their position—not necessarily approve of it, that's another question—but you could certainly understand it.

These are people who are being crushed and destroyed from every direction. If they grasp at some straw for survival, it's not surprising— even if grasping at that straw means helping to kill people like their cousins across the border.

That's the way conquerors work. They've always worked that way. They worked that way in India.

It's not that India was a peaceful place before—it wasn't. Nor was the western hemisphere a pacifist utopia. But there's no doubt that almost everywhere the Europeans went they raised the level of violence to a significant degree. Serious military historians don't have any doubts about that—it was already evident by the eighteenth century. Again, you can read it in Adam Smith.

One reason for that is that Europe had been fighting vicious, murderous wars internally. So it had developed an unsurpassed culture of violence. That culture was even more important than the technology, which was not all that much greater than other cultures.

The description of what the Europeans did is just monstrous. The British and Dutch merchants—actually merchant warriors—moved into Asia and broke into trading areas that had been functioning for long, long periods, with pretty well-established rules. They were more or less free, fairly pacific—sort of like free-trade areas.

The Europeans destroyed what was in their way. That was true over almost the entire world, with very few exceptions. European wars were wars of extermination. If we were to be honest about that history, we would describe it simply as a barbarian invasion.

The natives had never seen anything like it. The only ones who were able to fend it off for a while were Japan and China. China sort of made the rules and had the technology and was powerful, so they were able to fend off Western intervention for a long time. But when their defenses finally broke down in the nineteenth century, China collapsed.

Japan fended it off almost entirely. That's why Japan is the one area of the Third World that developed. That's striking. The one part of the Third World that wasn't colonized is the one part that's part of the industrialized world. That's not by accident.

To strengthen the point, you need only look at the parts of Europe that were colonized. Those parts—like Ireland—are much like the Third World. The patterns are striking. So when people in the Third World blame the history of imperialism for their plight, they have a very strong case to make.

It's interesting to see how this is treated in the West these days. There was an amazing article in the *Wall Street Journal* [of January 7, 1993] criticizing the intervention in Somalia. It was by Angelo Codevilla, a so-called scholar at the Hoover Institute at Stanford, who says: Look, the problem in the world is that Western intellectuals hate their culture and therefore they terminated colonialism. Only civilizations of great generosity can undertake tasks as noble as colonialism, which tries to rescue barbarians all over the world from their miserable fate. The Europeans did it—and of course gave them enormous gifts and benefits. But then these Western intellectuals who hate their own cultures forced them to withdraw. The result is what you now see.

You really have to go to the Nazi archives to find anything comparable to that. Apart from the stupendous ignorance—ignorance so colossal that it can only appear among respected intellectuals—the moral level is so low you'd have to go to the Nazi archives. And yet this is an op-ed in the *Wall Street Journal*. It probably won't get much criticism.

It was interesting to read the right-wing papers in England—the *Sunday Telegraph* and the *Daily Telegraph*—after Rigoberta Menchu [a Guatemalan Indian activist and author] won the Nobel Prize. They, especially their Central America correspondent, were infuriated. Their view is: True, there were atrocities in Guatemala. But either they were carried out by the left-wing guerrillas or they were an understandable response by the respectable sectors of the society to the violence and atrocities of these Marxist priests. So to give a Nobel Prize to the person who's been torturing the Indians all these years, Rigoberta Menchu....

It's hard for me to reproduce this. You have to read the original. Again, it's straight out of the Stalinist and Nazi archives—at their worst. But it's very typical of elements of British and American culture.

The roots of racism

All over the world—from LA to the Balkans to the Caucasus to India—there's a surge of tribalism, nationalism, religious fanaticism, racism. Why now?

First of all, let's remember that it's always been going on.

I grant you that, but it seems more pronounced.

In parts of the world it's more pronounced. Take Eastern Europe. Europe is altogether a very racist place, even worse than the US, but Eastern Europe is particularly ugly. That society traditionally had very bitter ethnic hatreds. One of the reasons why many of us are here is that our grandparents fled from that.

Up until a couple of years ago, Eastern Europe was under the control of a very harsh tyranny—the Soviet system. It immobilized the civil society, which meant that it eliminated what was good, but it also suppressed what was bad. Now that the tyranny is gone, the civil society is coming back—including its warts, of which there are plenty.

Elsewhere in the world, say in Africa, there are all kinds of atrocities. They were always there. One of the worst atrocities was in the 1980s. From 1980 to 1988, US-backed South Africa was responsible for about a million and a half killings, plus about sixty billion dollars worth of damage—and that's only in the region surrounding South Africa.

Nobody here cared about that, because the US was backing it. If you go back to the 1970s in Burundi, there was a huge massacre, tens of thousands of people killed. Nobody cared.

In Western Europe, there's an increase in regionalism. This in part reflects the decline of their democratic institutions. As the European Community slowly consolidates towards executive power, reflecting big economic concentrations, people are trying to find other ways to preserve their identity. That leads to a lot of regionalism, with both positive and negative aspects. That's not the whole story, but a lot of it.

Germany had the most liberal asylum policies in the world—now they want to limit civil liberties, and ban political parties.

There's a lot of talk about German racism, and it's bad enough. For example, kicking out the Gypsies and sending them off to Romania is a scandal you can't even describe. The Gypsies were treated just like the Jews in the Holocaust, but nobody's batting an eyelash about that because nobody gives a damn about the Gypsies.

But we should remember that there are other things going on too, which are getting less publicity. Take Spain. It was admitted into the

European Community with some conditions. One was that it's to be a barrier to the hordes of North Africans whom the Europeans are afraid will flock up to Europe.

There are plenty of boat people trying to get across the narrow distance between North Africa to Spain—kind of like Haiti and the Dominican Republic. If they make it, the boat people are immediately expelled by the Spanish police and navy. It's very ugly.

There are, of course, reasons why people are going from Africa to Europe and not the other direction. There are five hundred years of reasons for that. But it's happening, and Europe doesn't want it. They want to preserve their wealth and keep the poor people out.

The same problem is occurring in Italy. The Lombard League, which includes a kind of neo-fascist element, won a recent electoral victory. It reflects northern Italian interests. They don't want to be saddled with the poor people in the south of Italy. And they're concerned about the North Africans coming up from the south, drifting up through Sicily into Italy. The north Italians don't want them—they want rich white people.

That brings in the whole question of race and racism and how that factored into the relationship between the North and the South.

There has always been racism. But it developed as a leading principle of thought and perception in the context of colonialism. That's understandable. When you have your boot on someone's neck, you have to justify it. The justification has to be their depravity.

It's very striking to see this in the case of people who aren't very different from one another. Take a look at the British conquest of Ireland, the earliest of the Western colonial conquests. It was described in the same terms as the conquest of Africa. The Irish were a different race. They weren't human. They weren't like us. We had to crush and destroy them.

Some Marxists say racism is a product of the economic system, of capitalism. Would you accept that?

No. It has to do with conquest, with oppression. If you're robbing somebody, oppressing them, dictating their lives, it's a very rare person who can say: "Look, I'm a monster. I'm doing this for my own good." Even Himmler didn't say that.

A standard technique of belief formation goes along with oppression, whether it's throwing them in gas chambers or charging them too much at a corner store, or anything in between. The standard reaction is to say: "It's their depravity. That's why I'm doing it. Maybe I'm even doing them good."

If it's their depravity, there's got to be something about them that makes them different from me. What's different about them will be whatever you can find.

And that's the justification.

Then it becomes racism. You can always find something—they have a different color hair or eyes, they're too fat, or they're gay. You find something that's different enough. Of course you can lie about it, so it's easier to find.

Take the Serbs and the Croats. They're indistinguishable. They use a different alphabet, but they speak the same language. They belong to different branches of the Catholic Church. That's about it. But many of them are perfectly ready to murder and destroy each other. They can imagine no higher task in life.

The unmentionable five-letter word

It's a given that ideology and propaganda are phenomena of other cultures. They don't exist in the United States. Class is in the same category. You've called it the "unmentionable five-letter word."

It's kind of interesting the way it works. Statistics about things like quality of life, infant mortality, life expectancy, etc. are usually broken down by race. It always turns out that blacks have horrible statistics as compared with whites.

But an interesting study was done by Vicente Navarro, a professor at Johns Hopkins who works on public health issues. He decided to reanalyze the statistics, separating out the factors of race and class. For example, he looked at white workers and black workers versus white executives and black executives. He discovered that much of the difference between blacks and whites was actually a class difference. If you look at poor white workers and white executives, the gap between them is enormous.

The study was obviously relevant to epidemiology and public health, so he submitted it to the major American medical journals. They all rejected it. He then sent it to the world's leading medical journal, *Lancet,* in Britain. They accepted it right away.

The reason is very clear. In the United States you're not allowed to talk about class differences. In fact, only two groups are allowed to be class-conscious in the United States. One of them is the business community, which is rabidly class-conscious. When you read their literature, it's all full of the danger of the masses and their rising power and how we have to defeat them. It's kind of vulgar, inverted Marxism.

The other group is the high planning sectors of the government. They talk the same way— how we have to worry about the rising aspirations of the common man and the impoverished masses who are seeking to improve standards and harming the business climate.

So they can be class-conscious. They have a job to do. But it's extremely important to make other people, the rest of the population, believe that there is no such thing as class. We're all just equal, we're all Americans, we live in harmony, we all work together, everything is great.

Take, for example, the book *Mandate for Change*, put out by the Progressive Policy Institute, the Clinton think tank. It was a book you could buy at airport newsstands, part of the campaign literature describing the Clinton administration's program. It has a section on "entrepreneurial economics," which is economics that's going to avoid the pitfalls of the right and the left.

It gives up these old-fashioned liberal ideas about entitlement and welfare mothers having a right to feed their children—that's all passé. We're not going to have any more of that stuff. We now have "enterprise economics," in which we improve investment and growth. The only people we want to help are workers and the firms in which they work.

According to this picture, we're all workers. There are firms in which we work. We would like to improve the firms in which we work, like we'd like to improve our kitchens, get a new refrigerator.

There's somebody missing from this story— there are no managers, no bosses, no investors. They don't exist. It's just workers and the firms in which we work. All the administration's interested in is helping us folks out there.

The word *entrepreneurs* shows up once, I think. They're the people who assist the workers and the firms in which they work. The word *profits* also appears once, if I recall. I don't know how that sneaked in—that's another dirty word, like *class.*

Or take the word *jobs.* It's now used to mean *profits.* So when, say, George Bush took off to Japan with Lee Iacocca and the rest of the auto executives, his slogan was "Jobs, jobs, jobs." That's what he was going for.

We know exactly how much George Bush cares about jobs. All you have to do is look at what happened during his presidency, when the number of unemployed and underemployed officially reached about seventeen million or so—a rise of eight million during his term of office.

He was trying to create conditions for exporting jobs overseas. He continued to help out with the undermining of unions and the lowering of real wages. So what does he mean when he and the media shout, "Jobs, jobs, jobs"? It's obvious: "Profits, profits, profits." Figure out a way to increase profits.

The idea is to create a picture among the population that we're all one happy family. We're America, we have a national interest, we're working together. There are us nice workers, the firms in which we work and the government who works for us. We pick them—they're our servants.

And that's all there is in the world—no other conflicts, no other categories of people, no further structure to the system beyond that. Certainly nothing like class. Unless you happen to be in the ruling class, in which case you're very well aware of it.

So then equally exotic issues like class oppression and class warfare occur only in obscure books and on Mars?

Or in the business press and the business literature, where it's written about all the time. It exists there because they have to worry about it.

You use the term "elite." The political economist and economic historian Samir Amin says it confers too much dignity upon them. He prefers "ruling class." Incidentally, a more recent invention is "the ruling crass."

The only reason I don't use the word *class* is that the terminology of political discourse is so debased it's hard to find any words at all. That's part of the point—to make it impossible to talk. For one thing, *class* has various associations. As soon as you say the word *class*, everybody falls down dead. They think, "There's some Marxist raving again."

But the other thing is that to do a really serious class analysis, you can't just talk about the ruling class. Are the professors at Harvard part of the ruling class? Are the editors of the *New York Times* part of the ruling class? Are the bureaucrats in the State Department? There are lots of different categories of people. So you can talk vaguely about *the establishment* or *the elites* or the people in *the dominant sectors.*

But I agree, you can't get away from the fact that there are sharp differences in power which in fact are ultimately rooted in the economic system. You can talk about *the masters,* if you like. It's Adam Smith's word, and he's now in fashion. The elite are the masters, and they follow what he called their "vile maxim"—namely, "all for ourselves and nothing for anyone else."

You say that class transcends race, essentially.

It certainly does. For example, the United States *could* become a color-free society. It's possible. I don't think it's going to happen, but it's perfectly possible that it would happen, and it would hardly change the political economy at all. Just as women could pass through the "glass ceiling" and that wouldn't change the political economy at all.

That's one of the reasons why you commonly find the business sector reasonably willing to support efforts to overcome racism and sexism. It doesn't matter that much for them. You lose a little white-male privilege in the executive suite, but that's not all that important as long as the basic institutions of power and domination survive intact.

And you can pay the women less.

Or you can pay them the same amount. Take England. They just went through ten pleasant years with the Iron Lady running things. Even worse than Reaganism.

Lingering in the shadows of the liberal democracies—where there's this pyramid of control and domination, where there's class and race and gender bias—is coercion, force.

That comes from the fact that objective power is concentrated. It lies in various places, like in patriarchy, in race. Crucially it also lies in ownership.

If you think about the way the society generally works, it's pretty much the way the founding fathers said. As John Jay put it, the country should be governed by those who own it, and the owners intend to follow Adam Smith's vile maxim. That's at the core of things. That can remain even if lots of other things change.

On the other hand, it's certainly worth overcoming the other forms of oppression. For people's lives, racism and sexism may be much worse than class oppression. When a kid was lynched in the South, that was worse than being paid low wages. So when we talk about the roots of the system of oppression, that can't be spelled out simply in terms of suffering. Suffering is an independent dimension, and you want to overcome suffering.

Human nature and self-image

Is racism something that's learned, or is it innately endowed?

I don't think either of those is the right answer. There's no doubt that there's a rich, complex human nature. We're not rocks. Anybody sane knows that an awful lot about us is genetically determined, including aspects of our behavior, our attitudes. That's not even a question among sane people.

When you go beyond that and ask what it is, you're entering into general ignorance. We know there's something about human nature that forces us to grow arms, not wings, and undergo puberty at roughly a certain age. And by now we know that acquisition of language, growth of the visual system and so on, are part of human nature in fundamental respects.

When you get to cultural patterns, belief systems and the like, the guess of the next guy you meet at the bus stop is about as good as that of the best scientist. Nobody knows anything. People can rant about it if they like, but they basically know almost nothing.

In this particular area we can at best make some reasonable speculations. I think the one I've outlined may be a reasonable guess. It's not so much that racism is in our genes. What is in our genes is the need for protecting our self-image. It's probably in our nature to find a way to recast anything that we do in some way that makes it possible for us to live with it.

It's the same in the broader social sphere, where there are institutions functioning, and systems of oppression and domination. The people who are in control, who are harming others—those people will construct justifications for themselves. They may do it in sophisticated ways or nonsophisticated ways, but they're going to do it. That much is in human nature. One of the consequences of that can turn out to be racism. It can turn out to be other things too.

Take the sophisticated ones. One of the intellectual gurus of the modern period in the United States was Reinhold Niebuhr. He was called the "theologian of the establishment." He was revered by the Kennedy liberal types, by people like George Kennan. He was considered a moral teacher of the contemporary generation.

It's interesting to look at why he was so revered. I went through his stuff once. (There was supposed to be a chapter about him in one of my books—but the publisher thought it would be too arcane for the audience, so I didn't include it.) The intellectual level is depressingly low—you can hardly keep a straight face.

But something made him appealing—his concept of the "paradox of grace." What it comes down to is this: No matter how much you try to do good, you're always going to do harm. Of course, he's an intellectual, so he had to dress it up with big words, but that's what it comes down to.

That's very appealing advice for people who are planning to enter a life of crime—to say, "No matter how much I try to do good, I'm always going to harm people. I can't get out of it." It's a wonderful idea for a Mafia don. He can go ahead and do whatever he feels like. If he harms people, "Oh my God, the paradox of grace."

That may well explain why Niebuhr was so appealing to American intellectuals in the post-World War II period. They were preparing to enter a life of major crime. They were going to be either the managers or the apologists for a period of global conquest.

Running the world is obviously going to entail enormous crimes. So they think, "Isn't it nice to have this doctrine behind us? Of course we're superbenevolent and humane, but the paradox of grace...."

Again, if you're an intellectual, you dress it up and write articles about it. The mechanisms, however, are quite simple.

I suppose all of that is, if you like, part of our nature, but in such a transparent way that we can't seriously call this a theory. Everybody knows from their own experience just about everything that's understood about human beings—how they act and why—if they stop to think about it. It's not quantum physics.

What about the so-called "competitive ethic?" Is there any evidence that we are naturally competitive? Many proponents of free market theory and market capitalism say you've got to give people the ability to compete—it's a natural thing.

There are certainly conditions under which people will compete, and there are also conditions under which people will cooperate. For example, take a family. Suppose that whoever is providing the money for the family loses his or her job, so they don't have enough food to eat.

The father is probably the strongest one in the family. Does he steal all the food and eat it, so all the kids starve? (I guess there are people who do that, but then you lock them up. There's a pathological defect there somewhere.) No, what you do is share.

Does that mean they're not competitive? No. It means that in *that* circumstance, they share. Those circumstances can extend quite broadly— for example, they can extend to the whole working class. That's what happens in periods of working class solidarity, when people struggle together to create unions and decent working conditions.

That's true of the United States, after all. Take a look at the Homestead strike a century ago [when Andrew Carnegie locked striking workers out of a steel mill in Pennsylvania]. That was a period of enormous ethnic rivalry and racism, directed mostly against Eastern European immigrants. But during that conflict they worked together. It's one of the few periods of real ethnic harmony. They worked together with Anglo-Saxon Americans and the Germans and the rest of them.

Let me tell you a personal story. I'm not particularly violent, but when I was in college, we had to take boxing. So the way we did it was to spar with a friend, wait until the thing was over and go home. But we were all amazed to find that after doing this pushing around for a while, we really wanted to hurt that other guy, our best friend. We could feel it coming out—we wanted to kill each other.

Does that mean that the desire to kill people is innate? In certain circumstances that desire is going to come out, even if it's your best friend. There are circumstances under which this aspect of our personality will dominate. But there are other circumstances in which other aspects will dominate. If you want to create a humane world, you change the circumstances.

How crucial is social conditioning in all of this? Let's say you're a child growing up in Somalia today.

How about a child growing up two blocks from here in Cambridge? Just last summer a student at MIT was killed—knifed—by a couple of teenagers from the local high school. They were engaged in a sport that works like this: They walk around and find somebody walking the street. Then one of the teenagers is picked to knock the person down with a single blow. If he fails to do it, the other kids beat the kid who failed.

So they were walking along and saw this MIT student. The chosen kid knocked the student down with one blow. For unexplained reasons, they also knifed and killed him. The teenagers didn't see anything especially wrong with it. They walked off and went to a bar somewhere. They were later picked up by the police because somebody had seen them. They hadn't even tried to get away.

These kids are growing up in Cambridge—not in the wealthy sections, but probably in the slums. Those aren't Somali slums by any means, or even Dorchester slums, but surely kids in the more affluent suburbs wouldn't act like that.

Does that mean they're different genetically? No. There's something about the social conditions in which they're growing up that makes this acceptable behavior, even natural behavior. Anyone who has grown up in an urban area must be aware of this.

I can remember from childhood, that there were neighborhoods where if you went, you'd be beaten up. You weren't supposed to be there. The people who were doing it—kids—felt justified and righteous about it. They were defending their turf. What else do they have to defend?

It can't happen here—can it?

Huey Long [a populist Louisiana governor and senator in the early 1930s] *once said that when fascism comes to this country, it's going to be wrapped in an American flag. You've commented on tendencies toward fascism in this country. You've even been quoting Hitler on the family and the role of women.*

The Republican convention—fortunately I saved myself the pain of watching television, but I read about it—struck such chords that I began looking up some literature on fascism from the 1930s. I looked up Hitler's speeches to women's groups and big rallies. The rhetoric was very similar to that of the "God-and-country" rally the first night of the Republican convention.

But I don't really take that similarity too seriously, because the levers of power are firmly in the hands of the corporate sector. It'll permit rabid fundamentalists to scream about God and country and family, but they're very far from having any influence over major power decisions.

That was obvious in the way the campaign developed. They were given the first night to scream and yell. They were even given the party platform—it was pre-Enlightenment. But then when the campaign started, we were back to business as usual.

But that can change. When people grow more alienated and isolated, they begin to develop highly irrational and very self-destructive attitudes. They want something in their lives. They want to identify themselves somehow. They don't want to be just glued to the television set. If most of the constructive ways are cut off, they turn to other ways.

You can see that in the polls too. I was just looking at a study by an American sociologist (published in England) of comparative religious attitudes in various countries. The figures are shocking. Three quarters of the American population literally believe in religious miracles. The numbers who believe in the devil, in resurrection, in God doing this and that—it's astonishing.

These numbers aren't duplicated anywhere else in the industrial world. You'd have to maybe go to mosques in Iran or do a poll among old ladies in Sicily to get numbers like this. Yet this is the American population.

Just a couple of years ago, there was a study of what people thought of evolution. The percentage of the population that believed in Darwinian evolution at that point was 9%—not all that much above statistical error. About half the population believed in divinely-guided evolution, Catholic church doctrine. About 40% thought the world was created a few thousand years ago.

Again, you've got to go back to pre-technological societies, or devastated peasant societies, before you get numbers like that. Those are the kinds of belief systems that show up in things like the God-and-country rally.

Religious fundamentalism can be a very scary phenomenon. It could be the mass base for an extremely dangerous popular movement. These fundamentalist leaders aren't stupid. They have huge amounts of money, they're organizing, they're moving the way they should, beginning to take over local offices where nobody notices them.

There was a striking phenomenon in the last election—it even made the front pages of the national newspapers. It turned out that in many parts of the country ultraright fundamentalist extremists had been running candidates without identifying them. It doesn't take a lot of work to get somebody elected to the school committee. Not too many people pay attention. You don't have to say who you are. You just appear with a friendly face and a smile and say "I'm going to help your kids" and people will vote for you.

A lot of people got elected because of these organized campaigns to take over local structures. If that ties in with some charismatic power figure who says, "I'm your leader, follow me," it could be very ugly. We could move back to real pre-Enlightenment times.

There's also a huge increase in fundamentalist media, particularly electronic media. You can't drive across the country without noticing it.

That was true years ago. I remember driving across the country, being bored out of my head and turning on the radio. Every station I found was some ranting minister. Now it's much worse, and of course now there's television.

Hume's paradox

You've said the real drama since 1776 has been the "relentless attack of the prosperous few upon the rights of the restless many." I want to ask you about the "restless many." Do they hold any cards?

Sure. They've won a lot of victories. The country is a lot more free than it was two hundred years ago. For one thing, we don't have slaves. That's a big change. Thomas Jefferson's goal, at the very left-liberal end of the spectrum, was to create a country "free of blot or mixture"—meaning no red Indians, no black people, just good white Anglo-Saxons. That's what the liberals wanted.

They didn't succeed. They did pretty much get rid of the native population—they almost succeeded in "exterminating" them (as they put it in those days)—but they couldn't get rid of the black population, and over time they've had to incorporate them in some fashion into society.

Freedom of speech has been vastly extended. Women finally received the franchise 150 years after the revolution. After a very bloody struggle, workers finally won some rights in the 1930s— about fifty years after they did in Europe. (They've been losing them ever since, but they won them to some extent.)

In many ways large parts of the general population have been integrated into the system of relative prosperity and relative freedom—almost always as a result of popular struggle. So the general population has lots of cards.

That's something that [English philosopher] David Hume pointed out a couple of centuries ago. In his work on political theory, he describes the paradox that, in any society, the population submits to the rulers, even though force is always in the hands of the governed.

Ultimately the governors, the rulers, can only rule if they control opinion—no matter how many guns they have. This is true of the most despotic societies and the most free, he wrote. If the general population won't accept things, the rulers are finished.

That underestimates the resources of violence, but expresses important truths nonetheless. There's a constant battle between people who refuse to accept domination and injustice and those who are trying to force people to accept them.

How to break from the system of indoctrination and propaganda? You've said that it's nearly impossible for individuals to do anything, that it's much easier and better to act collectively. What prevents people from getting associated?

There's a big investment involved. Everybody lives within a cultural and social framework which has certain values and certain opportunities. It assigns cost to various kinds of action and benefits to others. You just live in that—you can't help it.

We live in a society that assigns benefits to efforts to achieve individual gain. Let's say I'm the father or mother of a family. What do I do with my time? I've got 24 hours a day. If I've got children to take care of, a future to worry about, what do I do?

One thing I can do is try to play up to the boss and see if I can get a dollar more an hour. Or maybe I can kick somebody in the face when I walk past them (if not directly then indirectly, by the mechanisms that are set up within a capitalist society). That's one way.

The other way is to spend my evenings trying to organize other people, who will then spend their evenings at meetings, go out on a picket line and carry out a long struggle in which they'll be beaten up by the police and lose their jobs. Maybe they'll finally get enough people together so they'll ultimately achieve a gain, which may or may not be greater than the gain that they tried to achieve by following the individualist course.

In game theory, this kind of situation is called "prisoner's dilemma." You can set up things called "games"—interactions—in which each participant will gain more if they work together, but you only gain if the other person works with you. If the other person is trying to maximize his or her own gain, you lose.

Let me take a simple case—driving to work. It would take me longer to take the subway than to drive to work. If we all took the subway and put the money into that instead of into roads, we'd all get there faster by the subway. But we all have to do it. If other people are going to be driving and I'm taking the subway, then private transportation is going to be better for the people who are doing it.

It's only if we all do something a different way that we'll all benefit a lot more. The costs to you—an individual—to work to create the possibilities to do things together can be severe. It's only if lots of people begin to do it, and do it seriously, that you get real benefits.

The same has been true of every popular movement that ever existed. Suppose you were a twenty-year-old black kid at Spelman College in Atlanta in 1960. You had two choices. One was: "I'll try to get a job in a business somewhere. Maybe somebody will be willing to pick a black manager. I'll be properly humble and bow and scrape. Maybe I'll live in a middle class home."

The other was to join SNCC [the Student Nonviolent Coordinating Committee, a black civil rights group of the 1960s], in which case you might get killed. You were certainly going to get beaten and defamed. It would be a very tough life for a long time. Maybe you'd finally be able to create enough popular support so that people like you and your family could live better.

It would be hard to make that second choice, given the alternatives available. Society is very much structured to try to drive you toward the individualist alternative. It's a remarkable fact that many young people took that second choice, suffered for it and helped create a much better world.

You've noted polls that indicate that 83% of the population regard the entire economic system as "inherently unfair." But it doesn't translate into anything.

It can only translate into anything if people do something about it. That's true whether you're talking about general things—like the inherent unfairness of the economic system, which requires revolutionary change—or about small things.

Take, say, health insurance. In public, almost nobody calls for a "Canadian-style" system. (That's the kind of system they have everywhere in the world—an efficient, nationally organized public health system that guarantees health services for everyone and—if it's more serious than Canada's system—also provides preventive care.)

And yet according to some polls, a majority of the population is in favor of it anyway, even though they've scarcely heard anybody advocate it. Does it matter? No. There'll be some kind of insurance company-based, "managed" health care system—designed to ensure that insurance companies and the health corporations they run will make plenty of money.

There are only two ways we could get the health care that most of the population wants. There either needs to be a large-scale popular movement—which would mean moving towards democracy, and nobody in power wants that—or the business community must decide that it would be good for them. They might do that.

This highly bureaucratized, extremely inefficient system designed for the benefit of one sector of the private enterprise system happens to harm other sectors. Auto companies pay more in health benefits here than they would across the border. They notice that. They may press for a more efficient system that breaks away from the extreme inefficiencies and irrationalities of the capitalist-based system.

"Outside the pale of intellectual responsibility"

Canadian journalist David Frum has called you the "great American crackpot." I think that ranks up there with the New Republic's *Martin Peretz placing you "outside the pale of intellectual responsibility." Frum also says, "There was a time when the* New York Times *op-ed page was your stomping ground." Have I missed something here?*

I guess I have too. I did have an op-ed once—it was in 1971, I think. This was the period when the corporate sector, and later the *New York Times*, had decided we'd better get out of Vietnam because it was costing us too much.

I had testified before the Senate Foreign Relations Committee. Senator Fulbright had in effect turned the Committee into a seminar. He was very turned off by the war and American foreign policy at that time. He invited me to testify. That was respectable enough. So they ran a segment of....

Excerpts of your comments. It wasn't an original piece you had written for the Times.

Maybe it was slightly edited, but it was essentially a piece of my testimony at the Committee. So it's true, the *Times* did publish a piece of testimony at the Foreign Relations Committee.

And that was your "stomping grounds." What about letters? How many letters of yours have they printed?

Occasionally, when an outlandish slander and lie about me has appeared there, I've written back to them. Sometimes they don't publish the letters. Once, maybe more, I was angry enough that I contacted a friend inside, who was able to put enough pressure on so they ran the letter.

But sometimes they just refused. In the *Times* book review section, there were a bunch of vicious lies about me and the Khmer Rouge. I wrote back a short letter responding, and they refused to publish it. I got annoyed and wrote back again—and actually got a response. They said they'd published a different letter—one they thought was better.

Other books by Noam Chomsky

This page and the next two list Noam Chomsky's political books and pamphlets in reverse chronological order (alphabetically within years). His books on linguistics aren't included unless they contain some political material. Addresses and phone numbers for smaller publishers are given the first time the publisher is mentioned.

Enter a World That Is Truly Surreal. Open Magazine Pamphlet Series (Box 2726, Westfield NJ 07091; 908 789 9608), 1993.

Letters from Lexington: Reflections on Propaganda. Common Courage Press (Box 702, Monroe ME 04951; 800 497 3207), 1993.

Open Fire (collection of Open Magazine pamphlets that contains Chomsky's *Media Control* and *U.S. Gulf Policy*). The New Press (NY), 1993.

Rethinking Camelot. South End Press (116 St Botolph St, Boston MA 02115; 617 266 0629 or 800 533 8478), 1993.

Year 501: The Conquest Continues. South End, 1993.

Chronicles of Dissent (sixteen David Barsamian interviews with Chomsky). Common Courage, 1992.

Stenographers to Power: Media and Propaganda (David Barsamian interviews Chomsky and others). Common Courage, 1992. (All the Chomsky material in this book is also in *Chronicles of Dissent* above.)

What Uncle Sam Really Wants (compiled from talks and interviews). Odonian Press (Box 7776, Berkeley CA 94707; 510 524 4000 or 800 REAL STORY), 1992.

Deterring Democracy. Verso (29 W 35th St, New York NY 10001; 212 244 3336), 1990; updated edition, Hill & Wang (NY), 1991.

Media Control: The Spectacular Achievements of Propaganda (transcript of a talk). Open Magazine Pamphlet Series, 1991.

Mobilizing Democracy: Changing the U.S. Role in the Middle East (with other authors). Edited by Greg Bates. Common Courage, 1991.

The New World Order (transcript of a talk). Open Magazine Pamphlet Series, 1991 (out of print).

Terrorizing the Neighborhood: American Foreign Policy in the Post-Cold War Era (based on a talk). Pressure Drop Press (Box 460754, San Francisco CA 94146), 1991.

U.S. Gulf Policy (transcript of a talk). Open Magazine Pamphlet Series, 1990 (out of print, but included in *Open Fire* above).

Necessary Illusions: Thought Control in Democratic Societies. South End, 1989.

The Culture of Terrorism. South End, 1988.

Language and Politics. Edited by C.P. Otero. Black Rose Books (distributed by the University of Toronto Press, 340 Nagel Dr, Cheektowaga NY 14225, 716 683 4547), 1988.

Manufacturing Consent (Edward S. Herman, principal author). Pantheon Books (NY), 1988.

Pirates and Emperors: International Terrorism in the Real World. Black Rose, 1986; new edition, Amana (Box 678, Brattleboro VT 05301; 802 257 0872), 1988.

The Chomsky Reader. Edited by James Peck. Pantheon, 1987.

On Power and Ideology: the Managua Lectures. South End, 1987.

Liberating Theory (with other authors). South End, 1986.

Turning the Tide: U.S. Intervention in Central America and the Struggle for Peace. South End, 1985.

The Fateful Triangle: The United States, Israel and the Palestinians. South End, 1983.

Towards a New Cold War. Pantheon, 1982.

Radical Priorities. Black Rose, 1981.

After the Cataclysm: Postwar Indochina and the Reconstruction of Imperial Ideology [The Political Economy of Human Rights, Part II] (with Edward S. Herman). South End, 1979.

Language and Responsibility (interviews with Mitsou Ronat). Pantheon, 1979.

The Washington Connection and Third World Fascism [The Political Economy of Human Rights, Part I] (with Edward S. Herman). South End, 1979.

Peace in the Middle East? Reflections on Justice and Nationhood. Pantheon, 1974 (out of print).

For Reasons of State. Pantheon, 1973 (out of print).

The Pentagon Papers, Volume 5, Analytic Essays and Index (edited with Howard Zinn). Beacon, 1972 (out of print).

Problems of Knowledge and Freedom (the Russell Lectures). Vintage Books (NY), 1972 (out of print).

At War with Asia: Essays on Indochina. Pantheon, 1970 (out of print).

American Power and the New Mandarins. Pantheon, 1969 (out of print).

Index

*Page numbers in **boldface** indicate major discussions (or relatively major ones, compared to the other citations in an entry). The alphabetization ignores spaces, hyphens and other punctuation marks.*

93

**The Real Story series
is based on a simple idea—
political books don't have to be boring.**

**Short, well-written and to the point,
Real Story books are meant to be <u>read</u>.**

*If you liked this book,
check out some of the others:*

What Uncle Sam Really Wants
Noam Chomsky

A brilliant overview of the real motivations behind US foreign policy, from the man the *New York Times* called "arguably the most important intellectual alive." Full of astounding information.

Highly recommended. —Booklist

Four stars. —Now magazine

My personal favorite. —Village Voice

> **32,000
> copies in
> print**

The Decline and Fall of the American Empire
Gore Vidal

Gore Vidal is one of our most important—and wittiest—social critics. This delightful little book is the perfect introduction to his political views.

Acerbic, deliciously, maliciously funny, and calculatingly provocative. —New York Times Book Review

The Greenpeace Guide to Anti-environmental
Organizations   Carl Deal

A comprehensive guide to more than 50 industry front groups that masquerade as environmental organizations. The deception is amazing.

Fascinating. A must. —New Orleans Times-Picayune